For Kathy—
Best
Stephanie

Additions and Subtractions

Poems by
Stephanie Kaplan Cohen

Stephanie Kaplan Cohen (signature)

Plain View Press
P.O. 42255
Austin, TX 78704

plainviewpress.net
sb@plainviewpress.net
512-441-2452

ISBN: 978-1-935514-58-9
Library of Congress Number: 2010932094

Cover art: "Expecting the Spring", oil on canvas, ©Vivian Wenhuey Chen. All rights reservedby artist.
Cover design by Susan Bright.

Acknowledgements

Grateful acknowledgement is given to the publications below for previously publishing these poems:
"At The Airport" in *96 Inc.*; "Benedict Molar," "Body Jumping" and "My Perfect Family" in *Westchester Review*; "Bird Feeder" in *Sierra Nevada Review*; "Burying Ground" in *Iconoclast and Parting Gifts*; "Catch a Break" in *Slant*; "Compliments," "Thanksgiving" and "Valentine's Day" in *The New York Times*; "First Grade" in *Spillway*; "If I Lie To You" and "Why This World Needs Liars" in *Talking River*; "It Was One A.M., The Hour Of Simply Nothing" and "What You Can Count On" in *Pearl*; "My First Car" and "Where Were You Last Night" in *Ship Of Fools*; "Never Mind The Mirror," "Winter of 1995" and "Pestilence War and Famine" in *Poet's Page*; "Osprey" in *Meridian Anthology of Contemporary Poetry*; "Places Everyone" in *Confluence*; "Seventh Birthday Party" in *Aura*; and "Thoughts On the Death Of An Ex-Husband" in *Split Verse Anthology*.

To Charles, again

Contents: Additions and Subtractions

My Perfect Family	9
Attention	10
At the Airport	11
The All Stars	12
Aidan	14
The Back Seat	15
Bird Feeder	16
April	17
Benedict Molar	18
The Burying Ground	19
Car Pool	20
Catch a Break	21
Clapboard House	22
Cognitive Dissonance	23
Come Back, Margaret	24
Compliments	26
Daisy Petals	27
Dark Days Of December	28
Definitions	29
Dreams	30
Elegy For an Ex-Girlfriend	31
February 28, 2008	32
Flashback	33
For Sylvia G.	34
Father's Day	35
Fortress	36
429 West Walnut Street	38
The Future	39
God Is Not a Woman	40
Golden School Days	41
The Golden Years	42
Haiku For Feet	43
Haiku For Funerals	44
Hold My Hand Please	45
I Am Waiting	46
I Dreamed Nebraska	47
If I Lie To You	48
It Was One A.M., the Hour Of Simply Nothing	49

Lament Of My Mother	50
The Last Day	51
The Last Of Day Of April	52
Laundromat Money	53
Letter To My Ex-Husband	54
Mad For You	55
March	56
March Twenty First	57
Martin	58
May Fifteen	59
Mom 1900-1990	60
Mother Chimney	61
Mother's Recipes	62
Mourning My Sister	63
My First Baby	64
Navigation	65
January	66
New Year's Resolutions	67
November	68
My First Car	69
Not Far From My House	70
Olfactory Hallucinations	71
Pain	72
Pestilence War and Famine	73
Places Everyone	74
Poetry Book	75
Possibilities: Good and Bad Ones That Is	76
For Rachel At Almost Two	77
Rachel In February	78
Rejections	79
Relatives	80
Rosh Hashonah	81
Sand Castles	82
Sayings From Rebecca	83
Sleep Deprived	84
So Where Were You Last Night?	85
Stephanie, You Stole My Soul	86

Stitches   87
Sweet Dreams   88
Suicide War   89
Sure Things   90
The Swimming Summer   91
Talk To Me Of Undergarments   92
Take a Chance   93
Thanksgiving   94
That Woman   95
To the Man Who Sits In Front Of Me At the Opera   96
2005   97
Valentine's Day   98
A Visitation   99
Wedding Recipe   101
Wedding Tree   102
When You Think Of Me   104
Why I Don't Write About It (The Cancer, That Is)   105
Satin   106
The Winter Of 2007   107
Working It Out   108
Why This World Needs Liars   109
Winter Truth   110
Wrong Number   111
Packing   112

About the Author   113

My Perfect Family

The world of my family
is the world. Some
don't like the politics
of some. Some don't
like the spouses of some.
Some don't like some.
They gather at my table
and I, the ignorant
know-nothing mother,
mother-in-law and
grandmother,
smile, tell them all
how happy they make me
in their love and devotion
to each other.

Attention

A bull gored me today.
Now that I have your
attention,
please take out the garbage.

Our children got tangled up,
and fell down the steps.
They are not in intensive care.
Please don't forget the W-2 forms.

The garage door sliced off
three of my fingers. Not. If you
don't fix it tomorrow, I will
chop it down.

At the Airport

Sitting, waiting for my flight to be called,
surrounded by mismatched carry-ons
I look up and see a glamorous lady.
Every hair is lacquered into place.
On her wrist, a gold bracelet matches
an equally impressive gold watch.
Her hands have long nails, and the
polish doesn't have one chip.

Looking at her,
I am a little girl
with ragged fingernails.
My blouse needs a tuck-in
and a sock is always sliding into the
heel of my scuffed oxfords.

I stare, and I hope that someday
I will look like that.
I forget that the time has come and gone.
That fancy lady who brings me back
to my grungy childhood
is probably younger than I.

The All Stars

There are many paths I might have taken
and many roads I could have walked.
When I allow myself a moment's doubt
I remind myself this is the only route
through which I could have acquired those jewels,
my children, their spouses, my darling grandchildren
and my children's new families, the in-laws.
All of them are such outstanding specimens
each one such a shining prize
that I have named them "The All Stars."
Every single festival, as I look around the table
so very full of my family, and my family's family
I tell myself how lucky we are
that they are all eager and willing to
grace our home for each and every special day.

Never a thought do those generous people give
to hours of holiday traffic,
shopping for a hostess gift,
and maybe a trinket for the kiddies
the need for a tie and jacket,
as they arrive early and often,
making themselves right at home,
going straight for the scotch and bourbon and gin
and vodka and brandy and beer and sherry
as I do a few last minute chores in the kitchen,
browning the Tofu for the vegetarian,
sizzling the steak for the carnivore,
boiling the pasta for the High Carb,
steaming the rice for the Yogi,
and peeling organic vegetables for the ecologist.

In the living room little children are happily running
and happily pulling everything off
every table that still has anything on it,
while the other grandparents, whose home this is not,
are calmly sipping their drinks and admiring the darling babies
whose abilities to make playthings out of almost nothing,
such as tents from wall hangings,
fencing weapons from fireplace tools,
and cars out of overturned chairs
is absolute proof of their superior intelligence.

Finally, we all gather at the table.
My husband makes the usual speech
blessing this day and our families
and each and every year,
as I lift my glass, I am
tired, cranky, and truly
grateful.

Aidan

Look you,
see that slim young man.
My first grandchild,
who used to be
my beloved Sarah.
We now must remember
to call him Aidan,
apologize when we say Good Girl.
We shop now for work boots
sport shirts and windbreakers.
I remember the prom dresses,
pleated skirts and twin sets.
Please, Aidan,
be as happy as Aidan
as you never were as
Sarah.

The Back Seat

Once again, it's my turn to ride in the back,
and I don't like it any more than I did
all those years ago
when I was a little girl
and ran a race with my sisters
to see who would win a place
next to the window.

The road stretched out for endless miles
until I grew up, jumped into the driver's seat,
sped away to college, dates,
and marriage.
Motherhood and wifehood found me
firmly ensconced in the front,
either as driver or co-pilot
listening to ferocious bickering,
occasionally mediating,
by seating one of the adversaries
up front next to me.

Very often now
it's not my chariot
nor that of my consort.
Those small passengers of mine
are the brawny new bosses.
They deposit us at airports and motels,
ferry us to restaurants in cities far away.
With studied good humor
I take my place in the back.
This time, I listen
to the secret song of the wind,
as I watch the odometer silently
clicking away.

Bird Feeder

It was inevitable
since we posted no rules,
welcomed all, from the plain,
to the fancy.
Sparrow, Woodpecker, Vireo,
Mourning Dove, Chickadee,
Nuthatch, Cardinal, and now
A not unhandsome bird,
since I've had a chance to look,
The Grackle, also known as
Starling, who has spread
The word to two or six hundred
of his buddies, and seems ready
to invade my turf with a few thousand
of their best friends.
And because I can't shut down
in this starving season,
I carry my umbrella to protect me
from my good deeds.

April

I've been watching
since November when
the leaves fell. Not all.
Some hung on,
lonely orphans, brown,
wind-tossed. More
fell in December,
but the fierce ones
stayed through January
and February snows.
Now it is time for
the greening buds,
and still, I see a few
shriveled reminders
of our last spring.

Benedict Molar

Oh, perfidious tooth, how I cared for you.
When young, did I not adorn you with silver.
And, as we grew together, thinking we would
never part, did I not fill you full
of purest gold,
hoping to soothe your middle-aged vapors.
And when you complained anew,
did I not go deep into your entrails,
extract the source of your pain,
provide cosmetic repair, a slipcover,
so that you remained as handsome
as the youngest of your confreres.
And for all of that, you ungrateful molar,
you showed no gratitude, but spewed forth poison,
until I finally knew you as my enemy tooth,
sentenced you and took you to the executioner.
Let this be a lesson to the rest of you.
Teeth, beware.

The Burying Ground

Each cousin can pay $100
to get the cemetery neat
or we can find $12,000
for perpetual care,
which is 750 each.
But some will not pay.
They have retired to
warmer parts,
and are not alarmed
at reports of
overgrown graves
and toppled headstones.
Others say if we pay
all the money now,
the cemetery bosses
will have no reason
to tidy further.
Still others insist
if we do not pay
our children never will,
and our parents will
lie in death,
as they never did in life,
in utter disarray.

Car Pool

Years ago five friends and I,
all wed to clones of the same man,
decided to stay married.

So, we formed a car pool.
When and if divorce beckoned
to all of us
at the same time,
we would take off for Reno.
Too many times
five of us were packed.

So to play it safe
we admitted three more women
and reserved
a nine passenger station wagon.
One day eight of us
were walking to that conveyance.

So, we delayed
and hired a bus
with forty places.
As of this morning
all the window seats
are taken.

Catch a Break

On Thursday
drifting snowflakes
turned into gold coins
as they landed.
Each coin became two
when we patted it.

The wind blew on Friday,
bringing with it fur coats
for all, made of recycled
plastic shopping bags.

Museums, theatres,
airplane rides
and hotel suites were free
on Saturday.

On Sunday, a warm voice
beamed us on the radio,
and told us how good,
how smart, how beautiful
we are.

A warm current of air
floated us to work on Monday.

Those who were hungering for children
conceived twins on Tuesday,
and a nanny came
to live with them.

Those who had children
were gratified to see
how good looking and brilliant
and grateful they had become
by Wednesday.

On Thursday it snowed again.

Clapboard House

I drive by a white clapboard house with a front porch,
and I want to be behind that door,
wearing an apron, waiting for the school bus.
I want my kids to come bouncing in,
dragging in, happy, sad, giggling, crying,
I want them to sit at my kitchen table.
You know the one. It's a big white enamel table,
with blue painted wooden legs.
I want them to tell me I didn't make enough cookies
as they take gulps of milk
fresh from the barn behind the house.
I want their father, my husband,
a weather worn, work worn farmer
to come strolling in, pat the boys,
kiss the girls on the tops of their heads,
and inquire as to the possibility of a cup of coffee
and the possibility of a few cookies
that I saved for him.
I want to walk over to the stove,
lift the pot cover, stir a little,
and know that my delicious hearty dinner,
enough for a mountain of men,
will be ready just on time.
I want the kids to go about their business,
practicing their instruments, doing their chores.
At dinner I want to serve up love and soup and laughter
At bedtime I want to turn into a wanton wife,
eager for the night.
I want to wake up early
to start the oatmeal, to start the coffee,
happy to start my new day.

Cognitive Dissonance

Cognitive dissonance is when
in the fitting room
trying on clothes,
I suck in my stomach

and strike a pose.

Suddenly I turn,
quite by mistake,
see an old woman

and do a double take.

Cognitive dissonance and I
had better shake hands.

Together, we will conquer
some very tough lands.

Come Back, Margaret

For the hearing aids
you did not get
when you were five.
Come back. Come back.

For the giggles of joy
you could not hear.
For the hugs and kisses
I still owe you.
Come back. Come back.

For the school they
did not let you finish,
and the boyfriend they
did not let you have.
Come back. Come back.

For the man who married you.
From the mother who said
Come back. Come back.

You did. You did.

For the girl you longed for
instead of the boy
you came home to birth.
Come back. Come back.

For your lover
when mother said
Canada is too far.
Come back. Come back.

For the sobriety you embraced
after your new husband
taught you to love
a little drink, a lot.
Come back. Come back.

For the love
your son gave away
to his grandmother,
to his cults,
to his girlfriends.
Come back. Come back.

To walk with friends
who cared when
you could only crawl.
Come back. Come back.

To die in your son's arms
after grandchildren's kisses.
To die in your own bed.
You come back. Please come back.

Compliments

When you tell me
with wonder in your voice
how great I look,
when you tell me
I am in amazing shape,
when you tell me
I walk with
youthful grace and verve
when you tell me
nobody would ever
guess my age
Do you know
how old I feel?

Daisy Petals

I forgive my mother.
I forgive my father.
Likewise, I excuse
ex-lovers, lovers
ex-friends,
ex-husbands.
I have learned to
accept,
sympathize
and even
empathize.
Now, may I
be excused.

Dark Days Of December

I call these the dark days, and I suffer them.
It is dark when I get up, and dark at tea-time,
if I were the tea-time type.

What saves these endless nights are brilliant days,
leaves laughing at me in their gala dresses,
dying with great showers of crisp goodbyes.

What saves these endless nights, with branches now bare,
are birds' nests, abandoned, visible, hanging on,
and waiting for maybe an early spring roomer.

What saves these endless nights are windows brilliant
with decorated trees and fancy candles, until it is time
to turn the page.

And be heartened by a different year,
With possibilities and the certainty
of lengthening days.

Definitions

Anger is the cover
of a boiling pot of lye.
Sad is an empty room,
only a small broken chair left.
Disappointment is a gift box,
tied with gold ribbons, opening to nothing.
Hate is a fingernail
eternally scratching the blackboard.
Disgust is an armful of live eels.

Dreams

I'm dancing.
My teeth are white,
my hair is long.
My thighs don't quiver,
my belly is flat.
I'm dancing with grace and daring leaps,
the jitterbug queen of the forties.

I'm dancing with all my old boyfriends,
the ones I liked
the ones who liked me,
and the ones I broke the rules with.
They all love me, every one of them.
They are young,
and also what they have become.

I get to choose again.
This time I make the choice I should have.
There are no detours for separations or rejections.
I choose happiness, love and success.

Now, it's almost over.
The wail of the trumpet has stopped.
The musicians are closing their cases.
What has happened is an unexpected riff.
I'm in love with my husband.
Instead of daydreams, I have nightmares.
I stay awake to count breaths.
A wry face makes my heart lurch
and I am just as young and scared
and unsure as any girl
in the first flush of romance.

Elegy For an Ex-Girlfriend

Old friend, old enemy, yesterday we were girls. Young women, but as I look at pictures, I see two girls, playing house, bending long slender necks with solemn joy, attending to babies, eating lobsters, drinking sangria, watching small children dare the waves. I remember morning phone calls, the trivial, and the not so trivial.

The comfort we gave each other at our parents' dying times. Once we shopped for black gloves, serious about the importance of correct mourning attire. By the time my last parent died, I wore red, and a flower in my hat. On that funeral day, I briefly wondered what you would think, but you were not there.

In spite of our unspoken love, I said. You said. My husband said and your husband said. So much did we say that as close as we had been, we drew a line, and separated that exact amount. When we saw each other, we looked with unseeing eyes. One day, when I was sick and walking crooked, I saw your car as you slowed down to look. Now, I thought. It will be as though the words had never been said, but the car picked up speed, and you drove away.

I heard about you, enemy dear. Our friends told me that although they knew I was not interested, they knew I would want to know that you were sick, so very sick. And even though they knew I was not interested, they knew I would want to know you were better, so very much better.

Until the day, the paper screamed at me that you were dead. Old friend, old enemy, I regret those words we spoke, and those words we did not speak.

February 28, 2008

I'm leaping into Leap Year, leap day. I'm jumping hopping, skipping into
The leap day of the leap year.

Why give the lousiest month of the year another day. I prefer to leap over,
not into leap day. I prefer to leap over leap day and the day before and the
twenty seven days before that.

Why can't we go from January to March. March One, March One-A, March
Two, March Two-A. I like to march. I like March. I prefer to march right
into March.

January brings with it the possibilities of a clean slate, a new year. Why then
does an extra long February suddenly show up calling itself a leap year. It
only has the nerve to do it once in a while, every so many years.

There's that word again. Stay home February. Get lost, February. Go away
February. Bury yourself. Dump yourself. Drown yourself, but get out of my
life. Stay out of my way.

Amen

Flashback

Who can invent the
freeze-frame so we
can be transported back to
moments of great joy
when life brings
what life always brings.

For Sylvia G.

When I see my good old friend
twenty years later
we are both good and old.

How are you, I'll say.
How have you been, I'll ask.
Fine and fine, she'll answer.
And you?
Splendid. Perfect. I'll say.

Then we will look at each other.
We will laugh the earthy laugh
we shared so many years ago
when it was too dangerous to cry.

Father's Day

You father you,
You daddy dear,
How could you know
what a father does.

Your father
never did
and maybe,
never loved.

You thought it was enough
to give piano lessons
pretty dresses,
and Sunday fun.

Later, when we three girls
were very good
or very pretty
we felt your love.

But, my daddy,
how much it would have meant
in the days of straight bangs
and a chubby body

If you had hugged me
told me you loved me
and promised me
a beautiful womanhood.

Fortress

I built with great care
a fortress.
I built it in spite of
relentless tides.

I built it to
house that fat little
Girl, who was the I,
with the straight
brown hair and
unsmiling face.

I hid
in a secret room,
the bad times,
the sad times,
the alone times,
the bad together times.

It is impregnable,
impenetrable,
except
for the peeking holes.

Holes, where the little I
looks out at the chosen few
who move through recess, always
chosen first.

Holes, through which my
children poke their fingers,
to show me where I failed,
where I am failing,
and where I will always
fail.

But here I am.
A deck of cards,
a fortress,
held together, after all,
by the secret glue of
the spirit,
Laughter.

429 West Walnut Street

Outside these walls,
in the yellow house next door,
a mother and a father
and their children
are having breakfast.
Orange juice, croissants
and hot chocolate.

Outside these walls,
in the shingle house next door,
sisters share a bedroom
and never fight.
They lend each other money
until the next allowance.
and give each other loose-leaf paper
all the time.

Outside these walls,
in the brick house behind us,
The mother and father
take the children to France.
They don't care
if the kids don't practice their scales.
And they go to bed
whenever they want.

How did I get born inside
these walls.

The Future

If someone were to ask,
I'd have to say, Body Bags.
Consider wars between countries,
wars between tribes,
wars between different religious groups,
wars of aggression,
wars of prevention.

Consider natural disasters,
earthquakes, floods, droughts.
Consider unnatural disasters,
boats sinking, airplanes falling,
bridges collapsing, buildings burning.
I tell you, it's a sure thing.
The future is Body Bags.

Who makes these things.
Are they stockpiled
somewhere safe
for those
who are not.
Do thy run out.
Is there a last year's style.
Are there special sizes
and prices
for children
and babies.

God Is Not a Woman

God is not a woman.
If there is a God
He is definitely
not a woman.
Sisters, who among you
would give children
terminal illness
and old people
interminable sickness.
Which one of you
would take the credit
for war, mutilation,
pain without end,
punishment without sin,
unending weariness,
hopelessness,
helplessness.

Golden School Days

September means
a new notebook
and a straight pen
to dip into the inkwell
on the scarred desk.

It means a dream
of a twirly ruffled skirt
that changes to
the navy box pleat, and a mother
with pins in her mouth.

It means a hope
of shiny Mary Janes
which become
brown oxfords
with sharkskin tips.

It means a wish
for a sister's golden curls
which turns into
a Buster Brown haircut
and two small clips.

It means
the same old me
back
for another year.

The Golden Years

You are old when
you refer to yourself
as older,
hate being called elderly
and the bus driver
gives you a senior discount,
without asking.

You are old when
almost everyone
looks familiar,
or just like someone
you used to know.

You are old when
you say, "I have
enough clothes
and stuff to last
the rest of my life."

You are old when
you renew your favorite
subscriptions for
only one year.

Haiku For Feet

Secret winter feet
are not half so pretty
as painted summer toes.

Haiku For Funerals

The woe of a great
funeral is one needs to
be dead to have one.

Hold My Hand Please

the way you held my hand
when we ran and
laughed through courtship.

the way you held my hand
as I groaned, pushed
and exalted at childbirth.

the way you held my hand
when we waved our last child
goodbye.

Now, hold my hand please
In the way which will tell me
there is nothing to fear
in the dark night ahead.

I Am Waiting

For midget, dwarf, albino, moron, idiot, transvestite, transsexual, homosexual, re-arm, unarm, disarm, pre-op, post-op, antibiotics, tranquilizers, sexualizers, pepalizers, organic, free-range, range-fed, radiation badges, sheriff's stars, preemies' incubators, nursing homes, rehab centers, euthanasia parlors, electric chairs, prize fights, football games, soccer matches, premenstrual, menstrual, and menopause

To be listed: Obsolete.

I Dreamed Nebraska

Was circumnavigated
by a board walk.

To the right, ramps led to
small towns with charming stores.

To the left, the railing separated us
from the sand the sea.

Of a certainty,
the corn is in the interior.

If I Lie To You

If I lie to you.
and reassure you that
you look beautiful
and amazingly young,
will you please
do the same for me,
maybe on the
telephone, where
our faces won't
give us away.

It Was One A.M., the Hour Of Simply Nothing

I wrote all the words
There were to write.
I ate all the food
I could contain.
Soft, warm, I lay
upon my bed, sinking,
deep through the sheets,
through the mattress,
the springs, the floor,
the cellar,
and me, I woke up in China.

Let someone else
make it rhyme.

Lament Of My Mother

I was the nobody,
the little middle.
Two older, two younger,
always quiet, always good.
No one ever noticed me.
I didn't matter.
But it was me.
It was me who
minded the store at night.
It was me who
carried my baby brother to the clinic.
It was me who
gave my mother the dimes I earned.
And nobody ever noticed.
And nobody ever hugged.
And nobody ever even kissed me.

The Last Day

The last day of
my mother's life,
her hand kept fluttering
to her face.
There were no words,
only that feeble gesture.

I finally remembered,
and removed one stray hair
growing from her cheek.
She smiled at me
and closed her eyes.

The Last Of Day Of April

April, my most favorite month,
in spite of Mr. Eliot
is leaving, and none too soon.
This year, April cheated,
gave us cold, winds, snow.
The fragile greens
timidly crept into view,
afraid to make bold display,
lest the April gods
showed their displeasure
with another freeze.

May, bless the robin
nesting outside my window.

Laundromat Money

The peach cost a quarter.
It glowed in a greengrocer's window.
Three times in two days
I passed it on my way to and from
the subway.
The fourth time,
I entered, pointed, and paid.
Outside, I bit into the
sweetness of desire,
the satisfaction of hunger.

With the taste still in
my mouth, my throat,
my heart, I went
home and washed towels
in the bathtub, singing.

Letter To My Ex-Husband

My once love,
at the end
were you still
so angry.

The arithmetic
of our entanglement
is a fierce equation.

Three thousand days
we spent together.
You had ten thousand days
after me.

Ten thousand days
for breaths to cleanse
and ten thousand nights
for dreams to blur the edges.

I wish
that when you lay dying
if you gave a thought
to us

you smiled
and patted the memory
of what we had hoped
to become.

Mad For You

I need a bedroom of my own
Where, if I choose
 I can turn on the light
at two o'clock in the morning
and read, sprawled diagonally
across the bed.

I need a kitchen of my own
where if I choose
I can cook eggs
three days in a row
for three meals in a row.

I need a room of my own
where if I choose
I can leave papers
scattered on the floor
and files stacked
in old cartons.

I need a tiny garden of my own
where, if I choose.
I can plant one rose bush,
one tomato plant
and lots of asparagus

I need a car of my own,
where, if I choose,
I can drive myself
straight back to
You.

March

Here it is.
Longer days of sunlight
on snow.
Here it is,
trying to be tough,
still winter.
In spite of itself,
quick stepping toward
the greening.
Willows know.

March Twenty First

Welcome sweet springtime
My sister Helen played, and then
the tune on the piano changed
to Happy Birthday. Helen, singing
lustily in her soprano,
Happy Birthday to me.

Happy Birthday to you
Dear Helen, I hope
you're having a ball,
a blast, I hope
they're tooting horns
for you, and your
death is filled
with joyous recognition
of your wonderful self.

Martin

Martin, if you had lived,
you would have taught
the People of Color
to walk with the
People of the Torah,
as they so often
walked with you.

May Fifteen

This is the week of the azaleas
and the peach trees.
The magnolias have dropped their
pale pink petals.
The rhododendrons are fairly bursting
with buds.
The mountain laurels bless us with
sparkling whiteness.
Tulips are still standing.
Daffodils gone.
Day lilies are in the wings.
The birds we fed all winter
have nested,
And babies are chirping.
I am made a child again
with all this wondrous beauty.

Mom 1900-1990

Augusta, I've owed you a poem
for as long as I have written poems.
Little girl, a blue eyed beauty with blonde curls.
Even that was not enough to get you noticed.
Born smack in the middle of a blue eyed blonde family,
you were just another girl, another mouth to feed.

Mad and sad little girl,
fought for the gold, the silver,
and never even got the bronze.
Mad and sad, wife, mother.
Augusta, how could you give
what you didn't have.

Augusta, should I say here
how you owned a millinery shop
filled with your creations.
Should I tell them
how proud you were when you
made enough money to buy a mink cape.

Augusta, should I tell them of the album
filled with photographs of you,
singing and dancing
half naked
When you starred
in the Senior Citizen follies.

How about the end.
I think it best, Augusta
To tell them you remained active and bright
Until the end, passing away
in the arms of your beloved family.

It's about time, she would say.
Tell it in two words or less.

Mother Chimney

Listen, you,
come down out of that chimney,
and I mean now. Or go back up.
So far, all you sent me
is two dead birds,
puny little things,
never would have been good for anything,
even when they were alive.
Take your bag,
and just take yourself
back out of that chimney.
And take your reindeer,
that are doing a dance on my roof,
and going to collapse
the whole damn thing,
that the roofer told me
might last a couple of years,
with luck.
Just take the whole damn show away
and go bother some folks
who have the time and money
for you and your bag of tricks.

Mother's Recipes

My mother said
"That's one for the books.
That takes the cake.
Control your emotions.
Pull up your socks."

My mother said
"I hate poor people.
Look at their mouths.
Their teeth are rotten.
They snivel and smell."

My mother said
"Why should I laugh?
When I was young,
I had hope.
Now, there is nothing."

My mother said
"You stole my money.
You stole my phone book.
You locked me up.
Help. Help. Help."

Mourning My Sister Margaret

The very next morning outside the window
I saw a humming bird
at the feeder.
Her head royal purple,
her body a shiny green.

She flew round and round the feeder,
long empty, looked at me
until I understood.

Sister, soar, fly,
swoop, drink nectar.
Love flowers, love life,
build nests,
sing to me, sing to me.

My First Baby

Oh baby, that was some baby.
Eight pounds, twenty-four inches,
and a stick of wood,
until the doorbell rang
or a dog barked.
Then, his arms and legs thrashed,
and his body quivered.
He howled and sobbed
with the fear
that filled us both.
It's nothing, they said.
It's something, I said.
Hypertonic, they said.
It's too much, I said.
He'll grow out of it, they said.
Not soon enough, I said
As I fought to dress, feed, hold,
love that baby.

Navigation

Now, our Bermuda Triangle years
have been navigated.
Now, we are delighted in our need
for each other.
Now, we nod as we read
each other's minds.
Now, we must practice a smile
when it is time to wave
Goodbye.

January

I resolve to try to keep peace in my heart.
I resolve to try not to hate any ethnic or religious group.
I resolve to try to stand straight and touch my toes every morning.
I resolve to try to avoid sugar and flour.
I resolve to try to keep my desk tidy.
I resolve to try to lose ten pounds,
and twenty years of grievances.
I resolve to try to say NO BIG DEAL
when somebody cuts me off in traffic,
I resolve to try not to make too many
Resolutions.

New Year's Resolutions

No more excuses.
2009 is the big one.
I hereby resolve to:
lose ten years,
gain perfect pitch,
grow six inches,
shrink my shoe size,
lengthen my fingers,
never to lose my temper,
always to be happy
and to love myself
just the way I am.

November

Each day shortens
as each leaf falls,
and wind chills.
I wait for snow,
ice, sleet, barren
landscape. Here,
we earn spring.

My First Car

There was one thing wrong with my first car.
It wasn't the color.
That was a black so deep
I looked into the hood and saw infinity.
It wasn't the dashboard.
That had so many buttons and levers
I knew if I could study the manual
that car and I would fly,
would pound through waves,
would study ocean floors.
The one thing wrong with my first car,
it came with my first husband.

Not Far From My House

Not far from my house
people still hang clothes
on tightly stretched lines

Clothespins secure blue jeans,
billowing white sheets,
shirts, pillowcases.

A woman stands
in bright sun
lifts her arms

and carries a wicker basket
of fresh air and sunshine
to her ironing board.

Olfactory Hallucinations

enrich my life.
They came with
the arrival of Brain Fever.
When it went, they stayed.
One day I sniff
sea air, strong and salty.
On the instant, I float
to my childhood beach.
Some days, not so sublime,
I catch the stink of
burning rubber which
no perfume can cover.
Mostly, they bless me
with baby powder, apples, lilacs,
with a stench thrown in
to remind me that
life, indeed,
is no bed of roses.

Pain

My firstborn yowled and howled
when traveling on the way to life.
I grunted, groaned, pushed,
all of me turned into a baby-making machine.
The doctor sitting at the tunnel,
The nurses standing by,
laughed at the remarkability of a baby
able to protest before birth.

The nursery named my first-born Screamer,
for that is what my baby did.
My baby slept a little,
nursed a lot,
and screamed evermore.

Many years have passed.
Nothing has changed.
With what secret grief
was my child
sent to me.

Pestilence War and Famine

Again, mothers are cradling their dead children.
Again, the youngest and strongest
leave us with a cheery wave,
and return, unmoving,
in their zippered cases,
or writhing
in those places built just for them
and their brothers
who fought in jungles
and in deserts
and their fathers
who fought for democracy,
and their grandfathers
who fought to end all wars.
In every corner of the world
we trip over dead bodies.

Places Everyone

At first we fed them, admired them,
made them welcome
with smiles and gestures.
Those foreigners had their ways.
Little children loved them, and to be fair,
they were a handsome bunch
until they took their welcome to mean
others like them could settle.
They made homes and begat.
A veritable parade of them,
stepping out of their assigned places.
It was intolerable, unsightly.
They made a mess,
grew quickly, flourished.
You know how it is
with their kind
who don't know their place.

We had no choice, really.
We were as kind as possible.
We allowed them no children,
and signaled they overstayed
by razing their homes.

It's unfortunate, but
It's just one of those things.
You know them.
They proliferate.
They poke around.
They mess, those
Canada Geese.

Poetry Book

I have a tattered book
of bad poetry hidden in
my dresser, under a
neat pile. A beau
gave it to my mother.
She presented it to
me, saying she knew
I loved poetry, but
I keep it because
I loved my mother.

Possibilities: Good and Bad Ones That Is

Exactly as my mother said.
You can dream anything.
And, she muttered,
it could always be worse.

Sam, reading a book at a friend's house, was companioned by their family
dog, who strolled over, nuzzled and asked for attention. Sam petted him.
The dog returned the favor by trying to bite off Sam's face.

It's been a warm autumn.
The leaves have hung on
in glorious color.

The Good News
Eyes untouched
Nose okay
Only a baby molar knocked out.
Sam's morale

The Bad News
One hundred and five stitches

In the It Could Be Worse Department, Sam's friend walked into a tree and
punctured his eyeball.

The light this time of year,
filtered through the trees,
has a magical quality.

Farmer's Almanac predicts a severe winter with periods of unseasonable
warmth.

For Rachel At Almost Two

I would dress you in silver.
I would gilt your sneakers.
I would put feathers in your hair,
fastened with a diamond clip.
I would wrap a boa around you,
hire a golden carriage
with four white horses.
I would decorate your cribby
with an ermine throw,
a pillow of finest satin,
and, I would learn your
language.

Rachel In February

I not going to Tinderdarden.
They is trotodiles in dere.
I have a secret for you.
They are toy trotodiles.
And I not going to Disney World.
They is trotodiles in dere.
Yes, but the trotodiles are under orders.
They are not allowed to bother the children.
Okay Stess, Lets go to Disney,
and ride on the trotodiles, right now.
Right now.

Rejections

When the
laundry basket was full
of my rejections,
I stopped saving them.

I try to think of rejections
as affirmations of
my intentions, persistence,
self-confidence, talent.

Then I crawl under
the piano, suck my
thumb, and cry.

Relatives

Relatives are a toothache
our tongue can't leave alone.
When it hurts the worst
We wish it gone.
And when its gone
we search emptiness
with relief,
then grief.

Rosh Hashonah

Gefiltes swim in my head
along with pot-roast gravy,
while I chop liver and mash eggs.

I dance to the popping cranberries.
peel oranges,
and pour cointreau.

Groats, bow ties and onions
jump into compliance
as Kasha Varnishkas.

My asparagus soldiers stand at attention
Without a whimper
As I peel them clean.

When I sit down with my family
I know I have made my
New Year prayer.

Sand Castles

The morning after the night before, that was the night of the wedding,
I woke up in the honeymoon suite of the hotel
where my wedding had transpired.
I woke and waited for calm assurance
that I expected after pre-nuptial angst.
What I got was post-nuptial angst.

I calmed myself. I told myself Bermuda would be better.
Bermuda was cold and rainy.
My husband had a tantrum. He needed sun.
A chill permeated my bones.
It found my heart, and there it made a little icy nest.
We moved on to Florida to catch the rays, to warm the body and the
spirit.

I consoled myself at the edge of the sea, making castles out of wet sand.
My husband spent the day oiling and rotating himself,
an Adonis on a self-timed spit.
When the sand castles were tall and the sun was low
that back I had turned to my husband, I had turned to the sun
was inflamed with the fire of the sun, the fire of ten thousand suns.

My husband advised more oil for the next day, fewer sand castles.
He advised haste. We were late for our dinner reservations.
My husband advised that he was hungry, that I was a crybaby.
I advised myself. I told that little icy nest in my heart not to mind.
I advised myself that this man, this husband, this well-lubricated Adonis
would someday be as a stranger to me.

Sayings From Rebecca

No kisses. No kisses Stessy. No kisses.
Seth, Molly, Emma and me, we know.
Grandmas' kisses are yuck.
They kiss so much wet.

Stessy, do you like my hair?
Me and Seth, we fixed each other.
I cut his, here and there and there.
And he cut mine, a little bit, everywhere.

For breakfast today, I'll have a popsicle
and ice-cream and three cookies too.
My mother would say yes.
Stessy, you know I'm joking you.

Stess, you have to take the crusts off.
Sandwiches with crust are too hard to chew.
There is only one crust I like.
The one on chicken is my very best.

Stessy, I'm drinking my milk now.
All of it is going down.
Watch my bones and teeth.
Am I getting so big and tall?

Car rides are too long.
Every time it's so too long,
and I'm so too tired and hot
and thirsty and hungry too.

Stessy, I miss you every day,
Every, every, every day.
No I won't, definite.
I won't talk to you
on the telephone.

Sleep Deprived

My routine has expanded.
After the usual ablutions, I apply
a special cream for the rash,
another for wrinkles,
a fancy one for dry spots,
medicine in the eyes,
on the toes,
pills for the bones,
another for tranquility.
By the time I'm ready
it's time to rise and
face another day.

So Where Were You Last Night?

Last night, last night.
As a matter of fact,
I am not sure
where I was last night.
It was one of those regular nights.
I stopped at Mac's just like
I do every night,
and in there I got to
talking with a bunch of the guys
just like I always do.
I remember putting a
little money down
on the game,
and I remember a couple
boiler makers, no more
than my usual,
and before You know it
I wake up, and where am I?
I'm in bed with
a terrible looking woman
with frizzy hair
and a beer belly
almost as big as mine,
and she's snoring.
I get up and get out
of there as fast as I can,
It's Canarsie
as I find out
when I go on the subway.
So where I was last night
is kind of a tough one.

Stephanie, You Stole My Soul

On the day before
You were born
I looked at death.
Not yet, I said.
I'm not ready.

The pains for which I was cursing you
and after three days of gut wrenching screams
for death to save me,
suddenly vanished with a cone of ether.
They took a knife
and carved you out of me.
They beamed when they
showed you to me.
She's a twelve pound miracle, they said.

I've never been the same.
When they took you,
they were not careful.
My spirit and dreams
went with you.

Stitches

I knitted you up, my mother dear.
I took every nice little thing
I could remember
and every nice little thing
I wished I could remember.
I puffed it up, and worked it round
until it became a soft coat of hugs
that enveloped me
with the mother love
for which I so dearly wished.

Comforted then,
I looked into
your china blue eyes
and saw
a wistful child,
hungry for kisses
that never came.

Sweet Dreams

Now I lay me down to sleep,
to toss and turn, mayhap to weep,
to twist the covers tight around,
to unwind myself, and lie unbound,
to pile up pillows, three or four,
to throw them all upon the floor,
to rise and seek a glass of milk,
to wonder, should I sleep on silk,
to pace the floor with angry thoughts,
to husband, who sleeps with snores and snorts,
to creep back in and trip on bed
to nurse my toe and watch the sky turn red.

Suicide War

Let's leave the children out of it.
since it is a war of suicide.
Let's say only grandparents
can go. We're ready.
We'll look really natty in uniforms,
need very little training
since our battle experience
will be searingly short.
We'll save the country
the expense of
geriatric care.
Two birds with one stone.

Sure Things

I am no longer sure of the sea,
and the sea was one of my sure things
along with sunrise, sunset and
my mother's shrill voice.

The morning tide roared its loneliness until
I threw on my one piece,
raced over the sand
and dove under the first wave.

I knew everything then.
How to deal with a rip tide.
How to get past the breakers,
How to swim to distant beaches.

Clamshells big as dinner plates
offered themselves, sharks teeth, snails,
all mine as I walked from my shore,
arms full of treasures,
home to my mother's shrill voice.

Now, hypodermics, tired prophylactics
and feces are the tidewash of the day.

I am no longer sure of the sea.
My mother's voice is a memory.
and I don't know a hell of a lot.

The Swimming Summer

I spent the summer swimming.
Swimming in a pool,
in the ocean,
swimming with memories,
desire and regrets.
Drowning in sorrow
for all that was
and all that might have been.

Talk To Me Of Undergarments

Underwear is the only ware
I do not ever, ever wear.
I keep my tits and tushy bare
because they need some good fresh air.

Take a Chance

Give yourself a chance,
the same one you
give to your
husband, your children.
Go on. I dare you,
give yourself a chance.
Go on and do it.

Give yourself a break.
The same one you
hand out so often.
Just turn it around,
give yourself a break
and understand, that
you too are human.

Every day, try to
like yourself a little more.
You are a rare specimen,
The only one of its kind,
and need to be preserved,
cherished, loved.

Thanksgiving

Well, God,
what have you got
up your sleeve for me?
You don't fool me with
good times.
You knew I had it
up to here
or there or whichever where
is too much

Here I am,
feeling so fine,
I even sing
in the car.

The husband, the kids,
the grandkids,
are all okay.
I'd tell you fine,
God,
but I know You
and your tricks.
The minute it looks
too good to be true,
it's too good
to be true.

That Woman

Not a chance.
I don't know that woman.
She has a sour look,
eyes, small and sharp.
Mean, I bet. And lines,
frowns etched deep
from nose to chin.
Does she never smile?
And that hair, so
obviously dyed.
Who is that woman?
Take that trick away
and bring a mirror.

To the Man Who Sits In Front Of Me At the Opera

For five years
I have watched you
escort your dates
to a night of culture.
One woman fell asleep.
I didn't see her again.
Some ladies lasted through
two or three performances.
Not one has
made it through
a whole season.
I'm starting to worry.
You're turning gray.
It's time for you
to give someone
a permanent subscription.

2005

This is the year
I suddenly discovered
I am married
to an old man.

This is the year
I suddenly discovered
my husband
is married
to an old woman.

Valentine's Day

February fourteen is the day of the
Great Marriage Compromise.
My husband, who
hates to shop, and even worse,
still doesn't know my size,
and maybe, even the color of my eyes,
will go to the local candy store,
and buy a fancy cardboard heart
filled with chocolates.
I will make a big to-do, and
he will grin with pleasure
and we will gobble them all up.
This box will replace
the box that has been on show
the year before,
and so on
and so on.

A Visitation

Uneasy, we sit at our kitchen table,
uncomfortable with so much room.
I hear echoes of laughter and crying
but all I see is shadows, and an old man
in whom I am mirrored.

We compete in the Grandparent Olympiad
timing how long each baby
allowed us to coo on the telephone.
We love our quiet routine,
and even know where the scotch tape
and magic marker are.

Until one special day they all arrive
tumbling from planes, jumping from cars,
bursting through the door, just as they
tumbled and burst forth from me
with innocent violent eagerness,
sure of their welcome.

The house rings with shouts of merriment and outrage.
Meals, usually Spartan are food feasts and food fights.
We walk carefully, head down, lest we trip
over a toy that has been carefully left
carelessly lying around in territorial assertion.

We wake to small children determinedly crawling over us
sticking fingers into our mouths and eyes.
The oldest announces, "We is hungry and we is thirsty."
We reach for a fresh diaper
thoughtfully left in a stack on our bed table.

continued...

No creaking bones then.
Quickly, we throw on bathrobes
tuck children under our arms
and start the day, which will
thrill, exhilarate and exhaust.

Just as we cannot bear the cacophony
another minute, they pack
their suitcases, tuck the toys back
in the attic.
Our children turn into adult strangers
holding babies, who wave good-bye.

Wedding Recipe

Take a lot of dough. Then double it.
throw in a few good eggs
like your cousin who lends the veil,
and your friend who introduces you to the wholesaler,
and your sister who slips you a pill
when all else fails.
Add plenty of nuts, like the floral designer
who wants to dye the roses black,
and your daughter, who wants to wear a strapless mini,
and the groom's mother, who wants filet mignon,
three thousand guests, and
who also wants to wear a strapless mini.
And the printer, who wants to do a four-color job
for the invitation.
And the band leader, who wants to fill the hall
with the sound of one hundred violins.

Go find the groom, who by this time
is hiding out and holding out
for his blue jeans and 1930's tuxedo jacket,
which, he says was good enough
when he was dating your daughter.

Keep quiet.
Tiptoe around oven lest cake falls.
Tiptoe around bride and groom
lest wedding fails.

After, enjoy it all, secondhand
through pricey photographer's eye.
Look what was going on while you were busy
tucking your daughter into strapless mini,
and squeezing groom's mother into strapless mini,
and sewing rip in groom's 1930's tuxedo jacket.

Finally, taste piece of frozen wedding cake
and savor exquisite balance of ingredients.

Wedding Tree

Let me explain.
I always wanted
my child to be married
under the Copper Beech.
Those red leaves and gentle branches
gave us a blessed canopy.

The Duck Pond, deserted
by Wood Ducks, now owned
by Canada geese, watched our labors,
strutted down our makeshift aisle,
finding it to their satisfaction,
slowly paraded back to their home,
to swim in stately circles.

The night before, in time old tradition,
we met to practice. Why do we need
to practice a wedding, anyway.

It wasn't rain. It was a deluge,
a torrent, A Noah's Ark flood.
We slogged ankle deep in mud
to that Copper Beech, laughing
a frightened nervous laugh
that hints of maybe a garage wedding.
Two of us buried knives,
a sure magic for rain to stop.

It did, and the skin of the earth settled back down.
The grass dried and the flowers stood up
The Copper Beech, leaves newly washed,
became a giant burning bush of a chupah.

And the drops of rain still left,
plunked softly down on us.
How could I know.
Those drops of water
if only I had tasted them,
were cosmic tears.

Years later, our beloved Beech
took sick. We called the
tree doctor. Time and again he injected
its silver bark with poisoned water,
the poison that can cure,
but our tree only
withered itself to death.

Then the news.
While our tree was dying
our child's marriage was
also in its last gasp.
We planted a Weeping Beech
where our good old tree
once stood.

When You Think Of Me

Please think of me
as I wished to be,
a column of steel,
with soft hugging arms,
keen ears, focused eyes,
smiling mouth.
Think of me,
knowing when to speak,
when to answer with silence.
Think of me laughing, rejoicing
in children and grandchildren.
Think of me as a person of
little malice, with small
and quick passing anger,
a person of limitless love
and understanding,
gentle with all creatures,
filled with wonder at natural beauty.
Please, for that is who I wished to be.

Why I Don't Write About It (The Cancer, That Is)

Because it's boring.
Because everybody
has written everything
about it.

Also, everybody
has sung, danced,
prayed, played,
acted it, embraced it
fought it and taught it.

Personally, I'd
just as soon
forget it, and
I'd have you
forget it.

If it works out,
the chemo, that is,
I have a lot of
living to do.

And if it doesn't,
forget
about this part.
Remember
the love and
the laughter.

Satin

Forever,
I have hated crows
with their black flapping
and loud song.

Today, I saw
elegant widows
wrapped from head to toe
in sleek black satin.

Their never ending
screams
are the sounds
that widows keep
deep inside.

The Winter Of 2007

The winter the ground was dry
and the temperature mild
we near froze to death.
Our bodies were storm filled,
storm tossed.
Our souls were pelted
with ice daggers.
Our hearts were tested
not by shovels of snow,
but marathons
of sleepless nights
and worried days.
Next year, I pray
the storms will rage
outside.

Working It Out

My trainer looks
Like Tom Hanks,
only younger.
My Pilates teacher
is the image of Cher,
only thinner.
So why do I
still have the
belly of Buddha.

Why This World Needs Liars

Liars are necessary.
How would we survive
without the promises
of a brilliant future,
a sunny life,
a wonderful spouse,
an ideal marriage,
beautiful children,
absolute health.

If the good fairy
leaned over the crib
and made us understand
just how hard it is
to get through
this living thing,
how many of us
would stick around.

Winter Truth

Snow is the perfect antidote
to the gaud
of spring and summer.

Freeze reminds us that steel
may melt, and an icicle
can pierce the heart.

Wrong Number

One friend I keep alive
by her telephone number.
Every now and then
I dial her,
and a nice woman
answers, and I say
I'm sorry I got
a wrong number, and
she says, No big deal,
and I want to tell
her what a big deal
it really is and how
glad I am that
a person like her
has my friend's number.

And then, I'll take
her out to tea and
find out that she looks
so much like my friend
did all those years ago
and we will be best
friends, almost and
it will be
like I didn't lose my friend
after all.

Packing

It's getting to be time,
time to get going.

It's time to pack my bags
with wishes and blessings.

It's time to empty my bags
of broken promises and old enemies.

Now, baggage free,
it's time to swim in the clouds.

About the Author

Stephanie Kaplan Cohen lives with her husband Charles in Westchester, New York. Her work has appeared in numerous literary magazines, university presses, anthologies and newspapers (including the *New York Times*). Stephanie is a proud member of the Authors Guild, and the International Women's Writing Guild.

She has held positions as an elementary education teacher, a medical social worker, a teacher/therapist of emotionally disturbed children in the public schools of New York City, a social worker in Family Court, as well as a desk clerk on a Commodity Exchange.

Additionally, Stephanie has enjoyed a life-long commitment to community service. She served as President of the Mental Health Division of Lexington School for the Deaf, President of Westchester and Putnam County Alzheimer's Association, and continues to write a column, "Ask Stephanie" for the Alzheimer's Newsletter. Stephanie served in numerous other volunteer positions, including vice-president of American Jewish Committee of Westchester and United Jewish Appeal of Westchester.

It was always Stephanie's ambition to become a published writer.

Stephanie and Charles are the parents of three children, three in-law children, and eight grandchildren, all of whom are all exceptional in all ways.

Breinigsville, PA USA
06 December 2010
250667BV00005B/1/P

9 781935 514589